www.fast-[illegible]/store.php

A FATHER'S EXPERIENCE : PARENTING TEENS

Copyright © Owusu Ansa Boafo 2010

All rights reserved

No part of this book may be reproduced in any form by photocopying or any electronic or mechanical means, including information storage or retrieval systems, without permission in writing from both the copyright owner and the publisher of the book

ISBN 978-184426-894-8

First published 2010 by
FASTPRINT PUBLISHING
Peterborough, England.

An environmentally friendly book printed and bound in England by www.printondemand-worldwide.com

This book is made entirely of chain-of-custody materials

Dedication

To present and future fathers and mothers,Mrs Mina Asantewah Boafo who graduated in 2004, my four children, Nana Abena Adoma Boafo, Opanin Kwadwo Boafo ,Maame Akua Anwaa Boafo and Nana Afua Nyarkoma Boafo ,uncle Justice Akuamoah Boateng, my sister, Grace Ntiriwah Boafo and Agona Family of Adansi-Asokwa in Ashanti Region of Ghana.

Also, in memory of my father; Opanin Kwadwo Boafo, my mother; Joanna Owusu Afriyie, my Grandmother;Yaa Nyarkomah of Adansi-Asokwa and uncle Osei Hyiaman Owusu Afriyie.

'Give me, Lord the courage to change those things that can be changed, the patience to bear those things that cannot be changed.

And the wisdom to know the difference`.

Prayer by Reinhold Niebuhur (1892-1971)

Contents

Acknowledgement

I would like to thank Almighty God for giving me good health and wisdom to get the ideas to initiate and complete this book.

I express my sincere gratitude to Nana Abena Adoma Boafo and Nana Afua Nyarkomah Boafo for typing the initial manuscript; and Maame Akua Anwaa Boafo for initial reading and Florence Ogunbowale who read the final manuscript and made very useful suggestions.

Any shortfalls are mine.

Foreword

This book was started in 2005 to share my personal experience with the present fathers, mothers and parents who are struggling and future ones who will struggle to bring up a child or children with special reference to teenagers in Britain.

Having brought up four children with my wife; I have realised the difficulties confronting parents, especially fathers, in bringing up teenagers in a 'liberalised' country like Britain.

The impact of `missing` fathers on children, in particular, those in their teenage years, the community, and lone parents form the central theme of this book.

Chapter One

Styles of Parenting

Some psychologists have put up a theory of distinguishing four types of parenting. They are authoritarian parents, uninvolved parents, authoritative parents and indulgent parents" (Martin 2005).

Authoritarian parents are more demanding but less responsive to their children's real needs. They are highly controlling but not very loving and warm. They expect their children to obey their instructions without explanation and might use emotional tactics to get their children to feel unloved, ashamed or guilty. They sometimes interfere when there are no issues or need to do so. Some of them resort to emotional or physical abuse when they are trying to control their off- spring.

Uninvolved parents with a laisse-faire attitude are permissive, understanding and set few clear boundaries. They do not monitor their children's activities. They are laid-back and are neither firm nor warm. For example, they allow their pre-teenagers to own televisions and play video games in their bedrooms.

Authoritative parents are fair and firm with their children. They set firm boundaries and they mean what they say. They keep close eye on them and give them support. They create enabling environment for their children to feel secure and happy.

Indulgent parents set few clear boundaries. They are permissive and undemanding, warm, loving but lax. Punishment is rarely carried through and their children appear to be in control of most situations.

Most real parents, according to Martin 2005, do not fit exactly into one of the four styles of parenting. Martin points out that parents who want their offspring to be content and happy should aim to love them for who they are and not who they would like them to be.

My style of parenting resembles Martin's Authoritative model. I try to create enabling environment in order for the children to feel secure and happy. I set firm boundaries and my word becomes my bond.

My children do not always react to this style of parenting favourably. For example, I always interfere with the type of friends they choose. I will make sure the friends are serious with their studies and they have supporting parents. Sometimes, this is not always the case. My teenage daughter had a friend whose attitude I did not like; but she insisted on befriending her. Her School started to send us letters about her behaviour at school especially in the classroom. The School reported that she arrives in class late and talks to a particular girl when the teacher is teaching. My boy wanted tattoos on his body. I disagreed with him. I informed him that it is OK and fasionable today. However, he could regret when he sees his body full of marks in future: and if he decides to remove them it could cost extra money and his body will never be the same. One day, he came to inform me that he wanted to pierce his ears. I was not for it. However, as a compromise, I discussed the issue with his mother. We agreed to let him have the piercing but I asked him what he would do if he went for an interview. He informed us that he would take them off. Our third child used to go out and come home late without informing us about her where about. It was a worry because there have been incidents of attacks on the streets of London on young teenage girls; therefore, I had to sit her down to discuss the implication of walking on the road at night on her own.

Chapter Two

My Moral Principles and Philosophy Based on Christianity

I have realised that Religious Education is important in raising children. I am a great believer in the moral education through the Holy Bible of Christianity. I was brought up in the Christian home; I attended Methodist Schools and a College run by Methodist Missionary in Africa. The experience helped me to adapt to my new environment when I arrived in Britain. Methodist Churches were far away from my residence. Therefore, I joined the local United Reformed Church (URC). Their preaching is similar to Methodism and I became an active member. I volunteered to be a Sunday school teacher when my teenagers were young.

I encouraged my children to accompany me to Church every Sunday. I secured admission at local Church of England Primary School for my four children. My son and the third child were able to gain admission into Church of England Secondary Schools.

During the christening of our son, the second child, the Minister asked me to choose a Bible passage for the occasion. I chose the following text for my son to read to the congregation:

Ecclesiastes Chapter 7 verses 13-25.I underlined the important verses in the text for him to be aware whilst he was reading the passage, verse 18 which says:

"...Avoid both extremes (in life)..."Verse 25"...I devoted myself to knowledge and study..."

I draw my children `s attention to any moral issue arose in the media, television and newspapers. For example, a poll commissioned by `JUST` 10 found that seven percent of 15-24 year- old had never heard of the 10 Commandments, the principles upon which Christianity is based (2004). The paper published the 10 Commandments. In case you have forgotten, these are:

1. Thou shalt love God.
2. Thou shalt not worship any other God.
3. Thou shalt not take the Lord`s name in vain.
4. Thou shalt keep the Sabbath
5. Thou shalt honour your mother and father.
6. Thou shalt not kill.
7. Thou shalt not commit adultery
8. Thou shalt not steal
9. Thou shalt not lie.
10. Thou shalt not covet others possessions.

I cut out and displayed the Ten Commandments in my kitchen above the washing machine for my children to read; even though they were taken to Sunday school when they were young. The boy and the third child took philosophy of religion and ethics as one of their 'A' level subjects.

Also, I found the teaching of the Chinese philosopher, Confucius stages of life relevant to my style of parenting. Therefore, I printed the sayings and displayed the celebrated stages of life in my kitchen:

'When I was fifteen, I was only interested in studying; when I was thirty, I began my life; at forty I was self – assured; at fifty, I understood my place in the vast scheme of things; at sixty, I learned to give up arguing; and now at seventy, I can do whatever I like without disrupting my life' Strathern (1999)

I emphasized the above guiding principles to my children especially during their teenage years. I advised them to equip themselves for the future and quoted Malcolm X saying that "Tomorrow belongs to those who prepare for it today "and the old adage of "knowledge is power". I usually tell my teenagers that if one has knowledge and skills and he or she is employed in a manual job with other people with no knowledge and skill; one day the supervisor might spot the one with the knowledge and skills through studying; and it is better to be 'addicted' to studies than illegal substances like heroin or crack – cocaine.

Chapter Three

Social Science Research Finding on Missing Fathers

The presence of a father or stepfather in a household is very important in raising children and teenagers. Their absence has detrimental effect on them in future according to Social Science Research findings.

According to Murray (2005), societies have been successful at making sure that almost all children come into the world with two biological parents committed to their care. Today, children still have a mother with them. However, there are growing number of children who have no father and who live in areas where hardly anyone has a father (Murray, 2005).

Academics for the Economic and Social Research Council have found that there are record number of single parent families in modern Britain; and half of Black Caribbean's, 4 in 10 Black Africans and 3 in 10 mixed heritages are brought up by a lone parent. This compared with 13 per cent of White Children, 10 percent of Pakistani, and only 5 percent of Indian or Bangladeshi babies (2004).

The social science finding states that girls without fathers tend to be emotionally damaged, they tend to search for father substitutes among young males which in turn increase the likelihood of repeating their mother's experience (Murray 2005). In general, boys without fathers tend to grow up unsocialised and they tend to have poor impulse control (Murray).

A 2001 Michigan University report showed that on the average, a father spends only sixty three minutes each weekday with his children, of which thirty three minutes are used up by family meals or watching television (2006). That means mothers are the one to bear the brunt of looking after and nurturing the child at home when the father is nowhere to be found.

Professor A.H Halsey (1993) has argued that "we're talking about situation of children born into single-parent families where the father never participated as a father…and from the missing father flows the missing community ethic". Professor Judy Dunn of Kings College University has pointed out that most pupils of single parent were particularly vulnerable to underachievement (2006)."It is partly the financial side but life is pretty grim for parents on their own, in financial terms and in dealing with their children's upset". Dunn (2006).

From my experience, boys in general do not take notice of most mothers at home, in terms of discipline. One day, I returned to the house late because of the traffic. When I opened the door, my wife screamed in excitement to draw my son's attention that I am at home; and I heard her saying to him that if he wants he can carry on with his indiscipline. His behaviour was similar to children without proper supervision at home and was like the proverbial saying "when the cat's away, the mice will play". I called my son and asked him what has happened whilst I was at work. He tried to explain the situation to me: and I realised that the young boy was just being naughty. I gave him strong warning and I advised him to listen and respect his mother as it is stated in the Bible.

When parents especially, the father fails to establish the ground rules before the age of six as the basis of discipline at home; it becomes too late to control a child when he or she is in the teens.

Boy-Child is active but idle in general with minimal house chores. Boys in general have the tendency to go out after school. Whenever my son returns home from school whilst I am at work; he will go out to play football with his friends. His mother might be preparing dinner in the kitchen but he will not volunteer to assist his mother. I devised a timetable for him and pasted it in the kitchen, which includes time for homework, housework and leisure activities with me and sometimes with his friends. My involvement with my children during the early and their teenager years is reflected throughout the book. It is hard to find time with the children but I realised that teaching them how to read, write and do basic Arithmetic can improve their Literacy and Numeracy skills. I therefore made a concerted effort to teach them how to read, write and do some basic arithmetic in their infancy and teenager years. I bought Mathematics book to practice in order to be able to guide them; and as a daily routine, I read at least fifteen minutes to them at bedtime.

Thus, the father or father substitute should be at home to play the role model for the children especially boy to emulate him. The father or father substitute should be somebody who has a caring and nurturing attitude. The absence of a father in a household has detrimental effect on him or her at a later stage of his or her life. Young children can copy bad behaviour from their friends outside the home; and it is the responsibility of the parent especially the father to impart some discipline in the home by setting boundaries for a child to adhere to it. In the absence of basic rules at home, the child can misbehave at school and in public places when he or she goes out to play with friends.

In the absence of the father, Matthews (2004), points out that criminals and drug dealers become heroes to impressionable black boys in particular because they have the power, the cars, the money, the bling and female attention.

Once a teenager, especially, a boy, chooses this line of life style, he becomes a 'macho' with different attitude towards life. He is anti-social, rude and disobedient to the rules and regulations of society and not a law-abiding citizen. A teenager with such attitude and behaviour cannot be contained at school; he or she will not settle and listen to his or her teacher. He or she may become the leader of a gang in the school and may be disruptive and disobey the school rules, which may lead to expulsion from school. They could become work-shy and therefore unemployable when they are of age to start to work.

Chapter Four

Conflict in a Marriage

My wife and I got married in Britain. Both of us were students with different aspirations and goals. I value the higher education system in Britain; therefore, I wanted to educate my self to the highest level.

To marry and study involved sacrifices, determination, patience, and perseverance.

Money or finance was a gargantuan problem at this stage of my marriage life; I have to work, go to College and come back to look after my children. This process was stressful for the family. Therefore, there were conflicts and arguments. I have noticed that in every relationship where the two people are from different backgrounds, there is bound to be conflict. Conflict is often thought of as always disruptive and negative, but Lewis Coser (1956) a sociologist, has argued that it can serve as venting social strains or clarifying group boundaries et cetera.

Amitai Etzioni (1993), one of the world's leading Social Scientists, has pointed out that both stable and unstable couples fight in any marriage; but the former couples fight better. That means, when two human beings meet, there is bound to be conflict in the course of their daily social interactions.

I remember one day I had an argument with my wife; and my third born knocked at the bedroom door to enter the room. She later wrote a note and dropped it on my table, saying "don't fight, daddy and mummy, I love you all" and added, "I wish I was not around when you are fighting". The content of the note dawned on me so I kept it. I realised that young children are very observant; therefore, I had to be mindful of my utterances and behaviour because it was a bad example for young children and teenagers living in a flat. Parents are the mentors and role models to their children; therefore, they should set good example for them to emulate in future.

As husband and wife are brought up in different environments, there is bound to be occasions when there is conflict; but that conflict should not lead to insults and abuse. The two of you met in the first place; therefore, you can resolve your day-to-day differences as you did when you were boy and girl friends. You can however, seek general advice from parents and close relatives.

Husband and wife should always remember the saying of Confucius,

"When anger arises, always think about the consequences".

When you have disagreement, regardless who is wrong, apologise. Say`, I am sorry I upset you. Would you forgive me? `Try to resolve your differences before you go to bed. Don't harbour a grudge the following day, rather move forward. God does not want us to look back that is why we have two front eyes.

In short, conflict is inevitable in any social interaction such as marriage. Celebrating their 78th wedding anniversary in 2006, Frank and Anita Milford point out that "an argument a day is the recipe for a long and happy marriage".

Marriage life has taught me that husband and wife need to respect each other, be faithful and honest to each other, transparent in their actions, work in partnership, communicate with each other and listen to each other's point of view because no one in this world has the monopoly of wisdom. Husbands and wives should teach by example to enable the child or children to emulate when they are ready to marry and have children of their own.

Chapter Five

Are You a 'Daddy' or a Father?

In the course of bringing up my children, I realised that there was a difference between being a father and being a 'dad' or daddy. I found out that in general, almost every male could procreate off spring with a woman to become a father; however, not every man could attain the informal title of a dad or daddy.

My argument is that `daddy involvement` in bringing up a child is paramount during all stages of a child's development. An ideal daddy should be a constant figure with the child from the time of conception till he or she has a child or children of his or her own and beyond. In summary, once a daddy the role of a daddy never stops, and parenting does not stop at teenage years either.

A daddy is always at home with the child or children after work. He should participate in the caring by changing the nappy, involving himself in feeding and putting him or her to sleep. A daddy takes keen interest in the child's day to day activities by reading to the young child or children, taking him or her to parties, shopping, parks, have interest in his or her education and also keen interest in their grand children. The needs of a daddy should be secondary to the needs of the child or children; therefore, the child's need should be the top priority.

Chapter Six

Who Comes First, the Child or Parents?

A Greek old lady advised me in the seventies that when I marry in future and I have a child, I should be careful of whom I give my child to look after. Her fear was that once you take a child to another house, and the door is shut or locked, one does not know what takes place behind closed doors.

Her advice to prospective parents is to keep their children in their homes (if possible) and look after them when they are very young. The mother or the father should stay at home till the child reaches the nursery stage.

As a result, when I married and I had a child, my wife and I decided to sacrifice for the child. Therefore, my wife stayed at home initially till the nursery stage and I engaged in full time work during the day in order to be able to keep an eye on the children.

I was able to train and was able to do a job, which allowed me some flexibility in the hours I worked. Hence, we decided to work day and night in rotation in order to make sure one person was always at home all the time in order to look after the baby and to supervise the children. In short, we placed the needs of our children first and our needs became secondary priorities.

All our children attended the Church of England Primary School. I got to know some parents as my children moved from one class to the other. I met the parents at the Parents Evenings, the Parent- Teacher Association meetings, Sports Days, School Fairs and Plays. The children made friends with their schoolmates; my wife and I made friends with some parents as well. The mother of one of the children, a single parent, lived on a nearby Housing Estate. She worked full time so she negotiated with us to pick her two young children to our flat so that she could collect them after work.

I was able to get to know the behaviour of the friends when we accepted some of them into our flat. We allowed them to play in an enclosed playing field. There was no apprehension as the children and their parents paid visit to our flat and accepted invitations to attend our children birthday parties and we reciprocated similar invitations.

The idea of our children sleeping over their friend's house or flat was not common with our first two children. It became a common practice with our last two children. We did not agree that young children should spend the night in the house of their friends. The apprehension was that each parent has different parental style in terms of setting different boundaries for their children to follow. Once a child and his or her parent became well known to us and accepted their style of parenting; there was no problem for our child to spend a night with his or her friend. In most cases, we are willing to allow the friend of our child to spend the night in our flat where we could supervise their behaviour.

Chapter Seven

Teenage Years in General

According to Oxford Concise Dictionary (1995), a teenager is a person from 13 to 19 years of age.

The word teenager from the point of view of Francis Beckett (2006) "came from the United States along with rock 'n' roll and it meant more than just being in your teens. It meant young people with some freedom and disposable cash, who could dress as they liked".

I noticed that the teenage period is a transitional period between childhood and adulthood that prepares one for mature social roles like work and marriage. It is period of high temptation and risk taking because there is high incidence of drinking alcohol and drug taking among children in that age group. Therefore, a teenager needs help and guidance to sail through this "turbulent" period of life.

Analysis showed that the main cause of teenage deaths is suicide, accidents, violence and substance misuse overdose. Also, criminal activity, aggression and promiscuity tend to peak during teenage and then declines. Lifestyles involving promiscuity and intravenous drug use can therefore expose a teenager to the Acquired Immune Deficiency Syndrome (AIDS) and other sexually transmitted diseases.

Parents have a duty to guide their children about the dangers of smoking, alcohol and illegal substances to delay or minimize their future intake by setting a good example and not buying too much alcohol in their weekly shopping. When the occasion arises especially if there is a newspaper article or a television programme about alcohol, drugs, teenage sexual activities, it is far better for parents to engage in an open and honest discussion about the dangers with the child or children. When my third child, a girl, completed her final year university examinations and came home; I gathered the four children and my wife .I congratulated the first two girls for not being pregnant during their secondary school and university years.

Peer pressure at this period of childhood development is widespread but if parents bring to a child's attention at an early age about the dangers of alcohol, smoking, drugs, he or she should have the confidence to say to his or her peer group that he or she might love to experiment but his or her parents would be angry with him or her. This gives them a way of saying no without being excluded from such group. It is a common knowledge that most of us have no idea what our teenagers are up to therefore; it is necessary to talk with them openly about life experiences and listen to them too.

When my second born, the only boy was in his teens, he came home one day and informed me that he wanted to tattoo his body. I informed his mother and later, I called him and sat him down and discussed the pros and cons with him. This is what I said: "Has any of your friends got tattoos on their bodies?" He said, "Few of them have". How many tattoos will you have? He replied: "I will have two". Which part of your body are you going to have them? "He replied. "I will have them on my arm and neck". I said to him that they are permanent markers and they are not easy to remove them. I referred to him what my mum and grandmother told me when I was in my teens with regard to fashion and personal hygiene. My grandmother advised me not to grow moustache in my adult years; and my mother was very particular about inspecting my armpits to see if there are hair and advised me to wash my armpit well whenever I have my bath. Her concern was that because of the heat one easily gets wet in his or her armpit and if I did not wash them properly it would smell. I said to my son that he would never know what he could become in future. I asked: "How will you cope with tattoos on your neck and arms if you become a `manager` or a Head of your Department in future?" He did not carry on with the 'fashion' after lengthy discussion.

A few weeks later, he asked me if he could pierce his ears. I sat him down once again and we talked about it. As I did not allow him to get the tattoo, I gave in to allow him pierce his ears after consultation with his mother. I asked him what type of earrings he was going to wear; he replied that there are special ones for boys and men. Well, the following week, I saw him wearing the earrings.

I later asked him, whether he was going to wear them if he was called for an interview. He had his ears pierced and wore the stud earrings. But since then, he graduated and is now working for a multi-national company. He no longer wears them because he has out grown the `fashion`.

When the thong underwear became fashionable, my teenager girls started wearing them. Therefore, I sat them down and advised them not to buy too many of them and they should refrain from exposing themselves when they wear them and walking on the street or in the public domain. I drew their attention that there has been public condemnation about the behaviour of some girls wearing the thongs in Ghana; and our relatives will disagree when they go on holidays in Ghana with them. With time, they minimized their purchase. Regarding the tattoos and the wearing of the thong underwear, I advised the children that whether they like it or not they cannot dress any how in a society they live in if they want to fit in with the general population. They cannot live in isolation from their teenage friends; that does not mean they have to `copy` blindly. They have to abide by the dress code of their future employers and for respectability by the populace. Fashion comes and goes therefore they should not follow it rigidly.

Chapter Eight

Family Structure Within Akan Culture of Ghana

'He that spareth his rod hateth his son: but he that loveth him chaseteneth him be times'.

(Proverbs chapter 13 verse 24)

I was born into an extended family unit in Ashanti, Ghana. I used to live in a compound house with my grandparents, cousins, uncles and `helpers`. Where there are no fathers` in the house, uncles and grandparents act as role models who become deterrent to mischievous teenagers in the household. In a typical Akan family, the grandmother is always at home to receive her grandchildren from school. In some households, there are always other people to give a helping hand to the grandmother in feeding and nurturing the off spring. When I was seven years of age in my hometown, my father was not around because he was a transport owner; therefore, he had to travel long distance. I lived with my uncle who was a teacher and then became my father figure.

My grandmother who was living in the house lived to the good age of 104 years. What I remember was that my mother was living in the nearby village and my grandmother was the one who was looking and nurturing four other younger grandchildren and myself. She was illiterate but fulfilled the potential role of a mother .She was at the house all the time with three female 'helpers'. She made sure that we were fed properly and my uncle supervised our homework and indirectly our behaviour.

When we reached our teens, my grandmother would sit in front of our house with her armchair during the night to deter us bringing any girls to the house (we were all boys). She made sure that we returned to the house at a specific time. If one of us was late, she gently queried why we were late and would make sure that we did not repeat that behaviour.

I remember one day I was playing football on the road with another young boy of my age. A man saw the two of us kicking the ball across the road whilst two cars were moving. The man ran to me and gave me a smack on my buttocks to stop me kicking the ball on the road. I ran back home to tell my uncle whilst crying. My uncle asked me the reason I was crying. When I explained, he too gave me a smack on my buttocks; and told me that the man was right because it is always dangerous to play football on the main road. I then realised that apart from my extended family looking after me, the community too was involved in my upbringing. This vindicates an old

African saying that "it takes a whole village to raise a child".

My culture allows a parent or an adult to smack a child if he or she misbehaves in the public place because we believe in the biblical teaching of 'spare the rod, spoil the child', Proverbs chapter 13 verse 24. I was smacked when I was playing football on the main road; and it did not affect me emotionally and psychologically because I have realized that the adult disciplined me with love at that time. I do believe lack of smacking children with love by parents has partly contributed to the indiscipline and anti-social behaviour among teenagers in schools and in the public places today. I smacked my older children when they were in their teens and were misbehaving and refused to respond to orders from me. I smacked them with love; it did not affect them emotionally. They were able to go to Universities and they are holding professional jobs now. They are not `angels` but they do behave themselves wherever they go and give respect to their elders.

Chapter Nine

Family Structure in Britain

Most sociologist point out that the `typical` family form has changed from extended to the nuclear or `modified` extended type in the British society (Dearlove and Saunders, 1986). With urbanisation, education and globalisation, nuclear family type has emerged whereby the wife, the husband and the child or children form the core family structure.

The first generation of Caribbeans and Africans arrived in the United Kingdom on their own accord. Therefore, they brought up their child or children in the nuclear family either with the help of their spouses if they are married or by themselves if they are single parents. I arrived in UK on my own with no grandparent to assist me in looking after my children.

When I settled to have a family of my own, I realised that the family structure was different from what I knew from Ashanti Culture. My wife and I have to apply our own styles of parenting. Moreover, our parenting has to reflect on the prevailing rules and laws of society.

We realised that childcare was expensive so I had to work Monday to Friday; and my wife worked nights during the weekends to cater for our two young children. She has to take them to school and I have to occupy them during the weekend and look after them at night. The part I played in nurturing and raising our four children is reflected throughout the book.

I did not have my mother around when I was young, but my grandmother played a leading role in my upbringing. Researchers from Cornell University (2005) have found that when children are going through adolescence, children of single mothers tend to do worse academically than those with married parents; but the problem can be alleviated if a grandmother or grandfather lives in the home. The presence of my grandmother in my household was the privilege I had during my teenage years in Africa. Our children did not have their grandparents around; therefore my wife and I have to fill the vacuum. We have to be around 24 hours especially before they started the Nursery and Primary School and the task of looking after them was shared mutually between us. It was an uphill struggle initially but it became part of our routine in the long run.

Chapter Ten

Quality Time and Bonding with My Children - Charity Begins at Home

I realized in my marriage that I had to spend more time with my children as there were no grandparents to assist in nurturing our children as I experienced and benefited during my childhood years in Africa.

With flexible working hours, I was able to pick my children up from school, attend parent-evenings with my wife and supervise their homework. During the summer holidays, they were taken out to parks and places of educational value in London. They had a planned summer holiday programme. There was a Borough reading scheme during the holidays run by the Borough libraries. Therefore, I encouraged the children to take part. They were given six books to read then at the end, the child takes the books to the library and the librarian will give them set of questions for the child to answer depending on the age of the child. Younger age groups could just draw a picture of how they understood the book; the older ones had to answer the questions in sentences.

I remembered my grandmother's style of parenting and I replicated it to my style of parenting. I made sure that I remained at home to see to the children returning from school when they were at secondary school. Meals were ready whenever they returned from school and we encouraged them to wash their hands after school and their plates and dishes after meals. When they were at nursery and primary schools, they were taken to school and were picked up by either my wife or myself.

Research in America has shown that the time between when children get out of school and the time when parents get home from work is the prime time for juvenile crime; it is also thought to be peak time for teenage sex. My wife and I therefore, made sure that one of us was at home to welcome the children from school when they became independent to go to school and return home by themselves. I emphasized to them the value of education in Britain, as they had no plot of land to go into farming as my parents did back home in Africa.

I set a good example by reading, studying, buying books, magazines and broadsheets of newspapers.

My dinning room is full of books and newspaper cuttings. I emphasized to them 'to marry' their books so that life could become less unbearable in this competitive and globalised world.

Time was set aside for their activities. For example, time table was devised so that time will be set aside for home work, television viewing, playing with toys and interaction with the children. Bedtime was set for 8.30pm when they were in the nursery and primary schools. As they reached secondary school levels, they were allowed to stay up till 9pm. They were encouraged to have a bath and brush their teeth before retiring to bed. Also, they were encouraged to iron their school uniforms, get their school bags and contents ready a night before.

I got involved in their school activities by volunteering to be a member of Parent Teachers' Association when they were in the primary and secondary schools. I assisted the schools to raise funds through summer and winter school fairs. By so doing, the teachers recognized me and realized that I took keen interest in my children's education.

I monitored the type of friends my children brought to the house. If I see a change in my child's behaviour after befriending a particular person, I discouraged them from playing with them. I remember that my grandmother would not let me play with a particular person if she saw that his behaviour would affect me in the long run. They got to know the likes and dislikes of what I wanted from their respective friends. Once a friend is accepted, the children feel free to bring them home. We got to know them and their families. I will initiate conversation with their friends when they come to the house. They informed their friends before they visit the house that I would interview them so they should be prepared to answer questions from me.

I listened carefully to the individual teachers at the parent evening when we meet subject teachers. I went with a notebook and jotted down the strengths and weaknesses of their subjects and their behaviour in the classrooms and on the playground. I was, and I am always interested in the children's behaviour in the classroom, as I have mentioned earlier.

I reiterated to them that the teacher's role is to teach and the child has to sit and listen to the teacher. They can speak when the teacher calls them to speak or answer any questions; or do not understand a concept and they want the teacher to explain to them. On this occasion, they can raise their hands and speak to the teacher.

My wife and I discouraged them from working when they were at secondary and sixth forms. However, when the first three children entered universities and took part-time work, we advised them to work on Sundays only so that they could have enough time to do their course work.

My children have become my best investment and my best friends; my relationship with them is always warm in tone, rich in communication and firm in discipline. I set good example for my children to emulate throughout their upbringing because they see me as honest, fair, open-minded and straightforward dad when it comes to moral values and discipline. These characteristics are reflected in the cards they design for me during Fathers Day and my Birthday.

When my third child, a girl, was twenty-one years of age, she used to go out but failed to contact home to inform her mum and I where she was and when she would return home. This was at the time of London terrorist bombing (2005), racially motivated attacks of a white man on the bus (2005) and a black teenage boy in Liverpool (2005).

She was therefore reminded that no one is preventing her from going out. However, we expect her to let us know where she is and most importantly to return home before 8pm. She was advised not to speak on the mobile phone when she is walking along our road to the house on her own at night. Somebody could be behind her and would not be able to see. I saw her one night talking on the mobile phone whilst I was driving home one night. I said to her that whilst her attention was on her mobile phone talking on the way home on her own at night; the chances are that somebody could molest her at night unawares. This is what I said when we got home: "Mame, did you know that it is very dangerous to speak on the phone in a quiet road like ours?" Her reply was that she does that all the time, and she did not think there was a danger to her.

I concluded by telling her that it is always better for her to walk straight home first and then make her phone calls at home or inform the person on the phone to call again at a later time.

Chapter Eleven

My Life Experience in Britain

I took the advantages of the higher educational system in the UK to educate myself by attending three former Polytechnics now Universities, namely Huddersfield, Kingston-Upon Thames, South Bank and Roehampton Institute of Higher Education in London. I had qualified as a psychiatric nurse so I was able to work part-time during the night while attending full time higher education during the day.

It was my desire to work in Personnel (Human Resources) in the seventies. I prepared myself for that by passing the professional examinations in 1981 and became a member of the British Institute of Personnel Management. I thought I could 'become what I wanted to be.'

However, in the late seventies and early eighties, it was an enormous uphill struggle to break into Personnel as a male Black African immigrant. I applied for personnel jobs in the public and private sector organizations, but I was turned down several times even though I had the British personnel professional qualification by examination.

I soon realized that to get a job, it is not what you know. Like most present generation of immigrant graduates, I was in catch-22 situation, where I could not get a job without experience, and cannot get experience without a job.

I was faced with quadruple oddity of being a first generation black African immigrant with an accent, having my initial education in Africa, my age and my 'double barrel' African names on top. Applying for a job, one has to state the educational qualifications starting from the primary education. Unfortunately and fortunately, I had my primary and secondary educations in Ghana-West Africa. On one hand, it helped me to learn self-discipline, how to spell, to understand the grammar and punctuation; on the other, it became a barrier in the job application process.

In 1998, The Independent newspaper stated that in a study of 11 blue-chip companies, the commission for Racial Equality (CRE) found that black candidates consistently fell at two of the three main hurdles in selection procedures: The main obstacles were encountered at the initial sift of application forms and the final assessment centre stage where groups of applicants are scored on a variety of exercises over a period of one or two days.

John Plunkett (2005) has pointed out that despite efforts to promote 'diversity' in the professions; it is still hard, for example for black and Asian talents to attract broadcasters' attention.

To quote Hardeeep Singh Kohh (2005), a writer, director and one of the stars of channel 4's Friday night sitcom, 'Meet the Magoons' there are difficulties in gaining employment in the media as an ethnic minority: "I have applied for jobs under my real name Hardeep Singh Kohli and under the name of Francis Ford. Using one of them, Hardeep Singh Kohli, I have been rejected, using the other name, Francis Ford, I have been invited in for a meeting the next day" (Kohli 2005)

Moreover, even today, Campbell and Roberts (2006) point out that 'despite efforts to improve diversity, research has found that the job interview can still be a major barrier to the fair selection of immigrant candidates'. 'The talk on trial' study (2006) carried out by Kings College London and the Department for Works and Pensions also found that job interviews often discriminate against people from ethnic minorities.

I realised that this was a vicious and never ending cycle and decided to undertake different courses whilst my children were young to gain insight into British society and the job market.

Eventually, I took a degree course in Social Sciences and a second degree in Sociology. Throughout my studies, I noticed that higher education placed me in contact with information and realised that a lot of information could be derived from the education sections of the broad sheets of the national newspapers.

In order to keep abreast with the education system in Britain, I started reading and buying different daily newspapers like the Guardian, The Times and Sunday Times The Telegraph and later The Independent on different days of the week. I visited the public libraries and photocopied articles on education and kept educational columns of the broad sheets. Through that, I was able to pick some good state secondary schools for my second and third children because there were no official statistics for the national school league tables in the eighties and early nineties. I cultivated the learning culture in my home for my children to emulate. I realized that the most important asset are my children therefore, they need the necessary support and encouragement to develop their hidden talents.

I found that there was a link between family income and educational achievement; therefore, I encouraged my wife to undertake further nursing courses in order to secure her position in the nursing profession. When my wife and I took interest in our educational advancement and our careers, it gave us the opportunity to give more help to our children to take advantage of good educational system in the country. We realised that as the children are born in Britain with all their education in the country and having no African accent, they stood a better chance of getting reasonable jobs in professional careers.

I opted for a job that allowed me more time with my children who at the time were, in primary school. I wanted to be around to take and collect them from school and to attend parent evenings.

When they entered secondary schools, I participated in the activities of the parent- teacher association too. The family, especially the children, became the key factor in my life as I planned my daily activities around their well-being.

To survive and cater for the children, I chose to work firstly in the social services and eventually settled in the social and nursing care. I specialised in the Addictive Behaviour field and I was able to do a course to Masters Degree level at St George's Hospital Medical School in London. I undertook a Certificate in Counselling at Roehampton Institute of Higher Education in London, which is now a University. It allowed me to work flexible hours during the day and night. It suited me greatly because it enabled me to place my children's needs above my own so that I could cater for their educational needs.

Chapter Twelve

Teenage Behaviours – Parental Responsibility

Parents need to be at the forefront in monitoring their children behaviour in schools. They should teach their children how to behave in the classroom, on the playgrounds and out of the school grounds.

When my children started nursery and throughout their primary and secondary education, we always told them to behave themselves. We emphasized to them about the importance of paying attention to the teachers in the classroom when they were being taught.

Children need to be quiet when teachers are talking and teaching in the classroom. They need to listen to teachers all the time. Teachers should be in control in the classroom and on the playing fields. The role of a child is to listen to the teacher so that he or she could teach the children.

When a fellow pupil distracts you by talking to you whilst the teacher is teaching, a child needs to put his or her hand up to draw the attention of the teacher. Failure to do so might put a child in trouble because by responding to a fellow pupil, the teacher might blame the child the teacher sees in the first place. To avoid such situation, that is why a child needs to pay attention to the teacher all the time whenever the teacher is talking or teaching.

A child has a playtime or break during the school timetable; therefore, a child can meet their friends or colleagues during playtime. Even during playtime, a child should behave towards his or her fellow pupil.

Because my children were aware that I did not subscribe to indiscipline, they tried to control themselves at school. To check what went on at school, I always asked them how the school day had been anytime they came home.

My last child returned from school one day, looking morbid. I asked her how she was that day; she was not forthcoming to give proper explanation. Upon further probing, she told me that, whilst in the ICT class, the teacher asked her to stand outside the classroom.

I queried the reason behind her punishment. Initially she informed me that she opened her pencil case and one of her pens fell on the floor and a friend next to her started to laugh and she fell as a result. Therefore, the teacher asked my daughter to stand outside the class.

Upon further probing, my daughter described into detail how she flicked her pen and it then landed on the floor. I then said to my daughter that the teacher was right to remove her from the classroom to allow other willing students to listen to the teacher. I was angry with her and stated that she was a form of distraction in the situation, and her rude behaviour and indiscipline was something I did not tolerate. I therefore warned her not to repeat that behaviour in the school and in the classroom again. I told my daughter that the punishment she received from the teacher was fair.

I noticed that my last child had the tendency to conform to her friends (she was the youngest in her year group). It came to our attention during parents evening that whenever the school bell rang for the change over of classrooms, my daughter would wait for her friends to go to the next classroom. By so doing, my daughter has been going to the next classroom late. Moreover, my daughter and some of their friends arrived in the classroom talking and making noise; and it took them sometime to settle to join other girls who are already settled to listen to the teacher.

My wife and I sat my daughter down and advised her against her behaviour and practice. We advised her to go to the next class on her own first and leave those girls to come on their own accord. At the end of the day, we emphasized to her that she would be blamed for her lateness and that would be placed on her school records.

At the time of writing the book my thirteen years old was attending all girls state school in London. The school has uniform policy. The girls should adhere to the correct uniform-code.

One day, a letter from her school arrived which had my wife's name on the envelope. My wife showed the letter to me; and the school reported to us that our daughter was late at school. Moreover, another day, she entered the classroom chatting with other girls and listening to her 'ipod' as well.

It is the procedure for parents to sign such letters and give the reply to the child to indicate that the parents have received it. On the letter, there was a space for parental comment. In the same week another letter arrived through the letterbox with her school logo. I opened it and I read another complaint. I said ' not again'. I was flabbergasted I said to myself, what could I do? My wife and I are trying to mould this 13 year old girl to conform to school rules; but we keep receiving complaints`, at one point, almost every week.

On this occasion, our daughter had a 'black band' around her hair instead of the usual 'red band'. That was against the school uniform policy. We thought we had devoted our time and resources to guide and support our daughter to be what she wants to be. But her disobedience towards the school rules and regulations were uncalled for.

The action taken by myself towards my daughter's insubordination in consultation with my wife was as follows:

I showed her the two letters when she returned from school; and I asked her to explain the reasons behind the content of the letters. About her lateness, she said she was late due to the poor weather condition (it was during the winter months). The letter stated that she was chatty and moreover, she was doing her homework in class and listening to her ipod on top. My daughter replied that the letter was a general one to students. She stated that she was not doing her mathematics homework; another girl was the culprit. She could not, however, give me a tangible explanation for having her ipod in her ears. She indicated that she was removing it when she entered the classroom. I did not believe her.

My daughter had planned to go out with her friends during that weekend. However, due to her disobedience in the classroom, my wife and I refused to let her go out during that weekend with her friends to watch a film. Also, her ipod was confiscated by me; and warned her not to take it to school. In addition, I informed her that I was going to monitor her closely from now onwards; and if she did not change her behaviour, we would deprive her of her benefits and privileges she received from us. For example, we hired a bouncy castle and she invited her friends to her house for her birthday. She was told that such treat would not be repeated if she did not change her behaviour and attitude towards her school rules and regulations from now on.

Chapter Thirteen

Talking and Listening to Teenagers

Listening is a skill many of us take it for granted- we all think that we listen to our fellow human beings when they are talking to us. Most of the time, adults are pre-occupied with their day-to-day problems that, we do not take the time to talk to and listen to our child or children,

Once a child reaches the school going age, he or she spends more time outside the home. Therefore, whenever they return from school, they have more information to share with brothers, sisters, mum and dad.

Teenagers of today are above their mental and chronological ages partly because they are exposed to the world event through the media (internet, computer, television, radio, newspapers, peer-group, magazines, family and neighbourhood) at an early age. Most of them are aware about their surroundings especially the girls. It is therefore fascinating to share with the experience of teenagers of today.

My last child, who is a thirteen-year-old, has become my best friend. She keeps me 'young' by telling me some of her experiences. . She knows I am interested in what happens in her school and the behaviour of her peer-group after school as well. She normally starts talking to me after school. Whenever I ask her what happens at school today; she will start 'you know what...' then says what she wants to tell me.

One day my daughter returned from school and informed me that a girl in year 10 who is 14 or 15 years old is married with a child. I asked her how she got to know. She said some girls were talking about it in school. I asked her opinion and she told me that she will not do that. She explained to me that the girl's religion allowed her to marry at that age. Her parents took her to her mother's country of origin to get married; therefore her parents look after her child while she is at school.

Another day she informed me that she had to ring 999 on behalf of a man who wanted the direction to the nearby Hospital, Accident and Emergency Unit. There was a man who was driving a van; and beside him was his colleague who fell ill. Therefore, the driver stopped near the bus stop where my daughter was waiting for the bus. The driver asked for the directions of the Accident and Emergency Unit. My daughter tried to direct him and according to her, since the man's command of English was not very good, she dialled for the ambulance on his behalf from her mobile phone. She told me that she was happy when the ambulance personnel arrived to take the man to Accident and Emergency Unit. However, I advised her to be careful especially when she is walking home alone and adults approach her; she should ignore them or run away and ring for the Police.

On another occasion, she informed me that the school raised some money with vouchers from Sainsbury, which parents sent to her school to redeem from the shop. The school received sufficient money to buy PE equipment for the department of Physical Education of the school. However, my daughter informed me that one Monday when they went to school, intruders had raided the PE department and had taken most of the equipment so they could not have PE lessons for the week.

My thirteen years old is more computer literate than most teachers who have taught me how to operate the computer. She teaches me the quickest way to operate the computer. I have to keep quiet and obey her instructions when she is teaching me. If I do not, she will refer to me that whenever I am explaining some basic mathematics to her and she did not pick up the concept quick enough, I normally become impatient. Therefore, I need to be a "good boy" and listen to her as a computer teacher. With her help, I have become more confident with the computer. I have realised that no one has monopoly of wisdom even though I am the dad and I teach my teenage daughter many things in life; I have also learnt basic computer operations from her. Therefore, children and teenagers need to be listened to and to be respected as well for their contribution in the family.

Chapter Fourteen

Teenage Years of My First Two Children

From the age of five, our first child, a girl, joined the tap dancing club and learnt to play the piano. When she was ten years old, she was sent to a boarding school in Ghana. We found that the education system in the eighties was not stimulating for the child, especially the state sector as we were living in the inner city of London. Her two aunties whilst in Ghana monitored her; and my wife and I used to visit her in Ghana. When she settled, she would visit us in Britain once in a year. She came to UK after seven years having completed her GCE and A levels, which enabled her to enter a university in the UK.

Her stay in Ghana has moulded her attitude towards life compared with the rest of the other children who remained in the UK. For example, she has formed the habit of washing most of her clothes with her hands on Fridays after work, and she gets involved in tidying up the house on Saturdays without being prompted to do so.

My second child is a boy. The education system in Ghana had changed by the time he was eleven years old. As a former British Colony, education system was formally based on the British education system. I took my GCE subjects conducted by the University of London and the West African Examination Council in Ghana; and the educational establishment in UK accepted these qualifications. The new system of education was not recognized in Britain. It would have been waste of his time if I had sent him to Ghana. Even the 'rich' people in Ghana were sending their children to UK during this period of `revolution` in Ghana's educational system. Therefore, he remained in Britain to have all his education.

From primary education until university, my wife and I had to work part-time during the weekend; and I had to work full time to enable us to have time for the boy. The two of us shared picking him from school and occupying him during the weekend and holiday period amicably. Unlike Africa, grandparents, extended relations and neighbours were not around to give a helping hand.

During the boy's primary school days, he became interested in football like most boys. He gained a place on six-a-side football team run by a young woman. Later, he joined the Mill Wall football Youth team. At secondary school, he was a member of the school team; although he was prone to injuries, he had a natural flair for the game.

Nevertheless, knowing his academic potential, I tried to discourage him from pursuing football as a career. Rather, I encouraged him to concentrate and put his faith in education. However, we noticed that being an all boys secondary school, the peer pressure was strong. He did not want to be a social outcast; he had more friends who were more interested in football, few were keen to study. It was an uphill struggle for my wife and I during our son's secondary school years.

We hired a tutor for him to come to our house to give him extra remedial lessons in science, his chosen GCSE subjects. To pay for the personal tutor, we had to make some sacrifices, forgo our leisure activities and our small luxuries above our needs. It was hard work for both of us. I had to learn the basic mathematics to be able to assist him at home as well. During his GCSE examination, I had to display his examination timetable on the notice board I bought for the children in our bedroom. This was to make sure that he went to the examination room fully prepared for the correct papers.

He achieved the required grades to be accepted in his secondary school to continue with his sixth form. He wanted to go to college for further education where some of his friends went; but I discouraged him from doing so. I found out that the college was too big for our son; he could join more laidback boys and adults who could distract him from concentrating on his books. At his former school, at least the tutors knew him, my wife and myself; and above all, it was a small sixth form school.

He was given the necessary support and encouragement. He continued to have a personal science tutor who came home once a week to assist him with biology and chemistry 'A' levels. He passed the requisite three 'A' levels subjects and was accepted into a former

Polytechnic, now a University in London to do honours degree in Life Sciences for three years. With support, he was able to pass the science degree with second-class honours; and now works with one of the leading multinational companies in U.K.

Chapter Fifteen

My Boy and His Primary School Days

One afternoon whilst I was waiting to pick my son up from primary school (he was ten years old), I saw some boys following another boy. I did not recognize my boy and it did not dawn on me that my son would be involved in a situation like that. I was surprised when I noticed that my son was being surrounded by black boys in the school (most of them were the friends of my boy).

I waited patiently for him to come to me but in vain. Then, one young boy came up to me and said; "excuse me are you waiting for Kwadwo?" the name of a male child born on Monday, in Akan – Ghana. I said yes, I was told that the boys are surrounding my son, and he is crying. I ran to the group of young boys. When I got there, my son started to cry. My son could not speak to me immediately. Rather one of his friends told me that the deputy head teacher (a male) of the school, also his class teacher, 'man-handled' my son when the head teacher returned to the classroom.

I was furious but I kept my cool. I went to the female head teacher to book an appointment for further information to see her the following day because the school had closed for the day.

When my wife and I went to see the head teacher and her deputy the following day, I presented my complaint to them. The head teacher tried to tell me what had happened the previous afternoon. In the final analysis, I was informed that the male teacher was out of the classroom that summer afternoon. When he returned to the classroom, the children were talking; therefore, for some 'reason' known to him, he held my son and pulled him. The deputy head teacher's excuse (he was the class teacher) was that, it was too hot that day; and he could not believe what he did. For some reason, the male teacher had to leave the school prematurely to another school in the South East part of London. He was instrumental in expelling at least two other ten – year old boys from the school for alleged misbehaviour.

From that experience, I decided to keep an eye and participate fully in the boy's education and his up bringing. My son's experience broke the camel's back. I became aware that the possibility of black children especially, a boy, attaining his educational goal was not fully propagated by that school. Therefore, I realized that it was up to the black parents especially (fathers) to take the lead, make sacrifices for the children's educational needs if these children are to fit fully into British society in future.

I soon realized that I have to make my son be aware that it is always possible for him to acquire a skill or educational qualification of his choice in Britain provided he has a guidance and support from me. Therefore, he should try to behave himself at school; he should obey the school rules and keep quiet all the time when teachers are teaching in the classroom. He needs to do extra work to succeed in his examination because there is no substitute for hard work when it comes to examination success. He was occupied as he was enrolled in a 5 – a – side football team when he was in the primary school. We also encouraged him to learn the piano too. He developed some skills in football that he played for Mill Wall Youth Team at the age of 10 years. He also ran for primary school team as well.

Chapter Sixteen

Special Needs of My Boy

When bringing up children, boys are special case. They are more active and most of them are boisterous; therefore, one needs to instil discipline and occupy a boy-child with lots of activities from the early years of his life.

I remember that when I was in the Primary School in Ghana, my grandmother took me to her son, my uncle, who had returned from Britain to stay with him. It is a common practice among Ashanti tribe for boys to be sent to their uncles to stay with them. The rational is that when boys are sent away to live with their uncles they become disciplined individuals in future. My uncle showed me how to clean the rooms, make bed, to polish the shoes, to cook basic food, make him cup of tea, wash small items of clothes and to iron them. I did some of the chores before I went to school. The ability to be able to undertake these daily activities and chores is important for future living. I attended a Day Secondary School and

I was able to transfer some of these skills in my day to day living. I had two years boarding experience too when I did two years Post -Secondary Teacher Training course at a Missionary College. The discipline I acquired at the Secondary school and College was exemplary and it moulded my life; and helped me to cope when I arrived in the Welsh countryside in Britain.

I included this chapter specifically for boys because of my own personal experience when I was growing up in Ghana as a boy. When boys are left unsupervised, they roam about with their friends. From an early age, some boys are focused in whatever they want to do; what they need is some guidance. However, other boys are easily influenced by their friends and become entangled with peer groups so they put pressure on them. If a boy falls within the latter group, then greater attention is needed for that boy-child.

Most State secondary schools in Britain are Day. When a boy returns home from school, most of them become idle with nothing to do (except their school home work even if they will sit down to do them). I was living on the Council Estate when my boy was young. The boys in the neighbourhood used to knock at the door to ask my son to play outside with them. I found that most of them were unsupervised; so I did not want my boy to associate himself with those boys.

I made sure that I knew some of his friends and their families very well. I did not encourage him to sleep over at the homes of his friends. Rather, his friends I knew very well were allowed to visit him at our house. I used to accompany them to football matches and take them out for a meal and he was allowed to return their visits.

Chapter Seventeen

My Boy's Secondary School Days

When our boy entered secondary school, he continued with football and was selected as a member of his school team. My wife and I would accompany their school team to various school matches to support him. He became obsessed with football and indicated his desire to pursue a career in football in future.

In his second year, my wife and I went to the parent evening; and his chemistry tutor informed us that our son had good understanding of chemistry. He explained to us that he set his class chemistry test without telling them to revise; and he scored a higher mark. I therefore, monitored all his activities. We supported him by employing a science tutor to come home once a week to give him extra lessons in Chemistry, Physics and Biology.

Even when he was sitting for his GCSE examination, I kept a copy of his examination timetable in my room to remind him which subject he had to do the next day or week.

He obtained above average GCSE results in the end and eventually his school accepted him to do the sixth form science course. He was able to pass 'A' levels and entered the university to pursue a science degree course. As I am very conversant with the education system in Britain through my personal experience and knowledge of the various educational columns of the broadsheets of the national newspapers, I acted as his career guidance and adviser. I encouraged him to do a degree course in life science because it could lead to various careers in sciences.

I had the belief that my son could become what he wanted to be (being a second generation immigrant) if he focused on his studies and with parental support as well.

Chapter Eighteen

My Boy, the Law and the Police

Whilst at secondary school, my son and five of his boy friends took a train from Clapham Junction to Victoria tube station after school. About thirty police Personnel were waiting for my son and his friends at the Victoria tube station.

They were interrogated at the station because the boys looked like some boys who had vandalized the train earlier on. My son was told that they had police report that two black boys wearing exactly the same clothes they were wearing had vandalized the train. However, when the police officers realized that they did not fit the description given to them; they set my son and his friends free.

I received a letter regarding the incident a few days later. The police stated that because our son had no criminal record, he was reprimanded; and set him free on that occasion. After the incident, I sat my son down and I advised him to be careful with the law and the police being a black boy.

I advised him that (since he was learning how to drive at that time) once he passes his driving test and gets a car, he should make sure that he gets the current insurance, MOT of his car; and he should carry them so that in case the police stops him he could show them. Then, he bought himself a Tigra Vauxhall saloon. He was stopped a few times at first. However, my son realized that once he had the relevant papers for the car, he had no cause to be afraid to drive his car around London. Also, he was advised to refrain from drinking and driving on the streets of London.

I advised him against the habit of loitering in the town or city centers with his boy friends especially after school. I told him that even as a grown up black man, whenever I enter big supermarkets, I become conscious that I am being monitored by the security staff. I become paranoid and I try to avoid entering into these big shops unless I am going to buy a specific item.

My personal experience makes me feel that the general misconceptions and assumption is that black boys and men like me have the tendency to shop lift; therefore, I advised my son at an early age to stay at home and sleep in his room if he has nothing to do after school or from work. He will be free from temptations if he occupies himself during the day and stops loitering around City Centres after school and during the night.

Chapter Nineteen

'What Life Has Taught Me'

As a guide to my teenagers, I produced a leaflet entitled 'what life has taught me'. I typed it out and distributed to my children and their close friends or any teenagers I come in contact with. I want to share the context with teenagers and adolescents wherever they may be:

Boy and girl friends

Teenagers should choose a boy or girl friend who are learning a trade or at college or university to pursue a career. They should choose their boy or girl friends with care; the person should be someone you share almost identical ideas with. They should get to know his or her background. They should be faithful to each other. They should, adopt the habit of 'giving and taking', and listen and communicate to each other. Then, when they are angry, they should always think about the consequences. They should always think before they speak even if they are angry. Failure to do that, they might regret if they react otherwise.

They should not marry until they have acquired or learnt a trade or have a skill or graduated and saved some money. They should marry at least when they are 30 years of age (if possible). To be successful in life depends partly on the type of friend's one make in ones teenage years and throughout ones adult life. Therefore, they should be your own separate friends because three of you cannot be friends; there is bound to be conflicts of interests and jealousy when three people are friends.

Education, training and careers

Teenagers should be multi-skilled, learn throughout their life and try to enroll with local college or university to learn a short skill or trade like catering/cookery, plumbing, electrical work, carpentry, painting and decorating, hairdressing, information technology in addition to their chosen careers. It is an age of life-long learning in the U.K. You have the chance to learn at any age; you should be able to inculcate education on the minds of their future children.

Work and Money

Teenagers should develop the discipline of working. They should live within their means and they should be credit-worthy because a good name is better than riches.

They should develop the habit of saving or putting some money aside for the rainy days. They should be aware of the saying 'look after the penny and the pounds will look after you'. They should not form the habit of borrowing money from their friends because it could generate into heated altercation or fight if the money is not paid in good time. They should not lend money to their friends. If their friends demand (£20) twenty pounds and if they have it; they could tell the person that he or she could have (£5) to keep; but they do not have £20 to lend.

Moreover, in this age of liberal loans and credit cards from the banks and finance companies, they should not go for loans, which are monies they had not worked for or earned it. Thus, they should not spend the money they have not earned because failure to pay the loan could lead to having their names being black-listed.

They should try hard to strive to be financially independent because if they have some cash in the bank then they could have peace of mind (and able to pay for their bills and look after themselves and their family in future.

Food and Diet

Young people should try to eat regularly; they should form the habit of eating breakfast and balanced meal a day. They should not go to bed when they are hungry. They should try to eat home-cooked meals to gain energy. They should learn to cook their favourite meal or breakfast and not to eat too much 'take-away'. They should eat more vegetables and cereals and try to avoid fatty or oily foods.

Fashion

There is no need to be scruffy nowadays. There are many budget shops to buy your shoes and clothes from. They should not become designer or 'logo' conscious girl or boy because fashion comes and goes, fashion goes round in circles. They should buy one or more fashionable clothes or items and shoe at a time because they become out of fashion. They should buy their designer clothes when they are on sale; and they should go to budget shops during summer and winter sales. As social being, one should dress to fit into the society she or he finds himself or herself in. Therefore, teenagers should always dress appropriately to conform to the generally accepted code of dress of society.

Alcohol, Drugs, Smoking, HIV and AIDS

They should drink alcohol in moderation if they are of age: however, if they do have a bad 'hang over', they should avoid taking them and avoid illegal drugs both soft and hard ones. They should not smoke because of the risk of physical and psychological effect on the body and brain.

Once they experiment with drugs especially heroin or crack- cocaine, anabolic steroids, they could ruin their lives permanently. They should not associate themselves with people who take and talk about alcohol and drugs. They should know that life can be enjoyable without alcohol and illegal drugs.

HIV/AIDS

They should be aware that it is an age of HIV/AIDS; therefore they should be careful with their sex lives. There is no cure for HIV/AIDS at the moment.

Reporting in the London independent newspaper (26/8/02), Nelson Mandela told a newspaper reporter in South Africa that he had lost three young relations in the

Eastern Cape to AIDS but had been asked by their close family not to reveal their identities. He gave this advice: 'All of us have to stand up and make sure that this matter is published'.

As HIV/AIDS has no respecter for mankind and has no cure at the moment, we all need to re-educate ourselves about the pandemic from time to time.

The Virus is transmitted:

1. Through sexual contact.
2. Through blood via blood transfusion or needle sharing.
3. From mother to child: a pregnant woman can possibly transmit the virus to her fetus or nursing mother can transmit it to her baby in her breast milk.

Therefore, only blood, semen, vaginal secretion and breast milk have been proven to transmit the injection to others.

NB: HIV is not spread by casual contact such as hugging and touching, by touching dishes, doorknobs or toilet seats, during participation in sports or mosquitoes. It is not transmitted to a person receiving blood or organs. However, it can be transmitted to a person receiving blood or organs from an infected donor. That is why blood banks and organ donor programs should screen donors and blood tissues thoroughly.

Those at risk of HIV/AIDS includes heterosexuals, homosexuals or bisexual men engaging unprotected sex, multiple sexual partners, intravenous drug users who share needles, infants born to mothers with HIV; and persons who received blood transfusions or clotting products between 1977 and 1985 in the UK (prior to Standard screening for the virus in the blood).

Prevention of AIDS requires foresight and self-discipline. Most experts still believe that HIV is principally transmitted by unsafe sex; and that people who suffer from other sexually transmitted disease (STD`s) are especially prone to HIV infection.

ABSTINENCE IS THE ONLY SURE WAY TO PREVENT SEXUAL TRANSMISSION.

Failure to do so one should take the following into consideration:

1. Do not have sexual intercourse with people known or suspected to be infected with the virus.
2 Do not use intravenous drugs. If intravenous drugs are used, do not share needles or syringes.
3 Avoid exposure to blood from injuries or nosebleeds where the status of the victim is unknown.
4 Anyone who tests positive for HIV may pass the disease on to others and should not donate blood, plasma, body organs or sperms.
5 HIV positive women should be counselled before becoming pregnant about the risk to unborn children.
6 Mothers who are HIV positive should not breastfeed.

7 `Safe sex` practices such as the use of latex condoms are highly effective in preventing HIV transmissions. However, there remains a risk of acquiring the infection even with the use of condoms.

8 HIV-positive patients who are taking anti-retroviral medications are less likely to transmit the virus.

It is very necessary for teenagers to take the precautionary measures seriously because it is always better to be safe than sorry. From a moral, ethical and legal standpoint, HIV positive carrier should warn any prospective sexual partner of their positive status.

Chapter Twenty

Teenage Years of My Last Two Children

My third child was born when I enrolled as a mature student at South Bank Polytechnic in London. She therefore had a brief nursery education at the former polytechnic student nursery. It was convenient for me because it enabled me to collect her after classes. When I completed my degree course, we got an admission at the local state primary school for her. It was a walking distance from our residence.

My wife used to work during the weekends; and I used to work the weekdays to cater for the needs of the children. She joined a gymnastics club and represented the inter-borough games competition. She was a member of her primary school athletics team and won few cups. I was involved in her school parent's teacher association activities, my wife and I used to take her and pick her up from various centres. She entered girl's secondary school and took part in the school plays.

Throughout her primary and secondary school days, she obeyed the school rules, listened to the teachers in the classroom and got on with her schoolwork. She was rewarded for her good behaviour and commitment at her school by appointing her as a deputy head girl in year 13. She was able to enter university to do three years honours degree in law and passed in July 2006.

There is eight-year gap between my third child and the last-born. Initially, I became relaxed in her supervision; therefore she was left off the hook in terms of discipline compared with the first three children. That was partly to do with the fact that I was tired after work and what I wanted to do was to be left alone.

She followed the footsteps of her older sisters and brother and attended the same nursery and primary schools. It soon dawned on me that being August born, she would always be one of the youngest in the class when it comes to secondary school transfer. Whilst majority would be already eleven years of age; she would still be ten years old.

She needed extra work to keep abreast with the rest of her class. I bought educational guides in English, Mathematics and Science from W.H. Smith to supplement her schoolwork. She was enrolled with the stagecoach the Art School. It was for children aged 4-16years of age. She was taught acting, singing and dancing. The experience gained assisted her to build herself confidence and to speak better. It was three hours every Saturday and she was with the group for three years.

A year before she was transferred to secondary school, she was given extra lessons in English and Mathematics to able to compete and sit for the Borough and outer Borough 11+ entrance tests. She tried the Grammar; Faith and Specialists schools entrance examinations. Eventually, she secured an admission into Girls Science specialist secondary school in the inner city of London.

She has already spent three years in the school. There have been trials and tribulations in terms of discipline in her school. Her science teacher in year nine contacted her mother to inform her that our daughter was rude. She informed us that one day she asked for her homework and my daughter retorted in a rude manner. I became flabbergasted and disappointed when the teacher informed me on the phone. I felt sad throughout the day because I realized my daughter had let me down in her behaviour at school.

She was in school when her mother and I received the message. When our daughter returned home, I called her sisters and brother and I asked her to tell us whether the science teacher was telling the truth. She was quiet and did not say a word. I informed my wife and the rest of my children that I am tired so they should handle the situation. The two older girls aged 28 and 21 years old respectively in 2006 were interested and agreed to discuss with their brother. On few occasions her brother has informed me that her young sister is rude. I delegated the task to them for her to realise the seriousness of her behaviour. They came to an agreement that their 'little' sister, that is what they call her, will be punished or disciplined for her misbehaviour. In the first place, they confiscated her ipod, mobile phone and the Internet; and did not allow her to go out over the weekend with her friends. She agreed to those rules and obeyed the directives from them with my backing.

With time, the boundaries were relaxed as her behaviour improved and they kept reminding her to refrain from repeating the insubordination when she returns to school. It coincided with summer holidays.

Chapter Twenty-One

Teenage Pregnancy

According to the BBC, Frank, Raising Kids (2005) almost 8,000 teenagers under 16 get pregnant every year in the UK. The latest statistics indicate that Britain "has recorded the highest rate to teenage pregnancies in Western Europe every year since 1980 and now has nearly twice as many births per thousand teenage girls as France; and three times as many as Sweden and Holland".

The research carried out in schools and church of Christian research across England adds to growing evidence of spiralling levels of sexual activity among children. The study concluded that 1:14 children, around seven per cent is sexually experience at the age of 13, one in 12 girls has asked for contraception at 14; and 1:4 girls has had sex by 16 (2005). The report pointed out that family and married parents can act as role models for the teenagers to deal with their sexual needs.

Children were much less likely to have sex in their early teens if they grew up with married parents. The study added 'parental example was hugely important and the role of father is a consistent factor in determining a child's success emotionally and interestingly intellectually' (2005).

When my first three children now in twenties were growing up, my wife and I emphasized to them the importance of education. We stressed to them that we are sacrificing for them in order to make them more secured living in Britain. Moreover, once they take their lessons and studies seriously and come out from college or university with a skill or marketable qualifications, they could compete with their counterparts or fellow age groups on the job market. We encouraged them to aim high because we are always there to support them.

I asked them whether any one of their friends have a child or children. My son informed me that two of his former schoolmates have children. When I asked if they are happy in their situation, he could not give an answer but commented that it will not be easy for them. He said, "Daddy, they are not going to School or College". My girls said to me that none of their mates have a child or children.

I said to them that I did not have a child neither did your mother when we were in our teens. Therefore, take us as your role model and mentor and focus on your studies.

One word of advice I have coined for my children who are still at secondary school and university is that 'they should marry their books', sit down to read their books, write and revise their work because there is no substitute to hard work when it comes to examination success.

I have produced a leaflet entitled "What life has taught me" and under HIV/AIDS (Chapter 19), I reiterated to them about the pandemic; and I drew their attention that Aids has no cure at the moment and it has become the world's most deadly infectious disease.

I always bring to their attention any national issue regarding sexual activity on the television and newspapers. I set good example by being faithful to their mother; and I try to abide by the marital vows of 'for better for worse'.

Whenever I was out of the house, I made sure that the children were aware, and apart from going to work, my movement was predictable. My social activities revolved around shopping, going to the street market to buy local foodstuffs or attending functions or meetings on Saturdays or Sundays. As a mentor and a role model, I have to teach them by example and show them that I do care and I am sacrificing for their well-being.

Throughout their teenage years, my wife and I made sure that the children's movements were monitored as much as possible. For example, we made sure that we know their friends and their families. The idea of the children 'sleeping over their friends' house was not in their lexicon because we are always suspicious of what happened behind closed doors whenever we left our children in the house of strangers. We however, allowed them to visit their close friends and relatives. These friends and their families are well known to both of us.

My thirteen years old daughter came back from school one day and informed me that during the Personal Social and Health Education lessons (PSHE) ten young mothers aged seventeen years came to the school with their mothers to talk to them about their experiences of being young mothers. She told me that the girls gave birth to their babies when they were thirteen and fourteen years of age.

The ten girls were shared among other year group. Her class had a girl who was once in their school. She had her baby when she was thirteen years of age. She informed me that the girl told them about her experiences of labour and when I asked her whether she advised them to follow her footstep; she told me that she advised them to continue to study till they finish their education and settle with a skill or qualification.

Her mission was to advise the girls to stay at school till they were old enough to become pregnant and have babies.

She regretted her decision to have a child and stressed that the young girls should not follow her example. They should not follow her example-she regretted. She said she was lucky that she had a supportive mother who looked after her baby and allowed her to continue with her education. She said she was seventeen and she was studying at a college and learning a trade.

I asked my daughter: "Are you going to follow her footstep and have a baby?" My daughter replied: "Daddy, don't say that to me, I will never do that". I said to her: "Good for you".

The School put on this kind of event to remind the girls to focus on their studies because life is not easy if you have a child in your teens. My wife and I told our daughter that the event was excellent because young girls of today need reminding of teenage pregnancy and its consequence.

Chapter Twenty-Two

Alcohol – Tobacco - Cannabis – Cocaine Use In Society

Eighty four percent of 12 year-olds have drunk alcohol according to the BBC Frank, Raising Kids (2005) and by the age of 16, ninety-four percent of young people have tried it. A European school project has found that more than a quarter of British teenagers had been drunk 20 times or more, the second highest level in Europe (2006).

It is a common knowledge that beverage manufacturers have come out with flavoured fruity alcoholic drinks such as alcopops. For example, my teenage boy and girl were seen with such a drink and when I checked the bottle, I realized that even though the bottle looks like a beverage drink, it has some alcohol in it. They were counselled and advised to be careful with such drinks because it is an indirect way to introduce teenagers to alcoholic drinks. I cautioned them by saying: "Do you know that what you are drinking has high alcohol content?" My son retorted: "Yes, I know". My daughter just said: "My brother offered me, so I could not refuse".

Alcohol is legal but it leads to violence and it is a frequent cause of road accidents; and it is involved in more than half of all visits to orthopaedic admissions and accident and emergency departments (Stuttaford, 2006).

Marijuana (Cannabis) is a substance, which had been down graded from B to class C recently (2005). That means society assumes that the substance is relatively harmless. Therefore, its use by the public is more relaxed and the police is liberal in its approach when someone is seen smoking a small amount, compared with the hard substances like heroin or cocaine which are Class A drugs. It has been noted by Dr Thomas Stuttaford (2006) that most medical experts accept that up to twenty five percent of people may carry genes that make them vulnerable to cannabis, a vulnerability that may lead to psychotic breakdown. Mark Henderson (2006) writing in the Times quoted a study that when a teenager uses cannabis that might open a biological `gateway` to more serious drug addiction later in life. The use of cannabis is blamed for acute heart problems, road accidents and some malignancies (Stuttaford, 2006).

A European school survey has found that a total of thirty eight percent of British

Teenagers had used cannabis (Dobson et al 2006). According to Government report (2006) twelve percent school pupils aged between 11 and 15 years old smoked cannabis; and it can be argued that the increase was as a result of the Government decision to downgrade cannabis from B to Class C. The decision to reclassify cannabis can also be argued that it has sent mixed messages to the youth about drugs.

Tobacco is another legal substance but it causes sixty percent of drug-related fatalities and forty percent of all hospital illness.

Cocaine use is on the increase and the spokesperson for Europe Against Drugs, Brett (2006) has pointed out that the increase in cocaine use is seen as fashionable and the media reports on the alleged use of hard drugs by some celebrities send out confusing messages to teenagers about drugs.

Professor Henry (2006) has pointed out that one cannot take cocaine and get away from it because regular cocaine users end up with little holes in their brain.

Parents are role models to their teenagers; they watch, listen, and observe our behaviours directly and indirectly at home, school, on the television and in the public places. The use of these substances by adults should be curtailed if possible to enable our teenagers to grow up to adulthood without the influence of illegal or legal substances.

These substances are addictive when taken in the first instance especially cocaine, marijuana as they all affect the nervous system. Once a teenager sees their parents

Smoking and drinking, what do we expect? They too will follow the footsteps, copy the adult, buy these substances or steal them from parents who smoke without knowing. Therefore, parents need to be discreet when they are drinking and smoking. If possible, they should avoid using them altogether so that our teenagers too would refrain from them.

Teenagers always copy from their significant others, therefore parents and extended family that take illegal and legal substances need to refrain from taking them.

The experience I have gained in addiction field has given me an insight into the Illegal Substance Culture. I have learnt a lot from the clients who come to my unit for detoxification programme. I have realised that addictive behaviour has no respecter for anybody irrespective of age, colour, race, class, gender and wealth. I always have empathy for the client groups especially those in their twenties because these children could have been my own.

If I see any newspaper article on Substance misuse, I will cut it and share the contents with my children. I tell them that both legal and illegal substance are widespread: they are found in the homes, in the Clubs, on the streets, in Schools, Colleges and Universities. They should be cautious with their new friends.

My conversation with my children on illegal substances has led them feel free to express their views and share their ideas with me. Any time my children tell me that they are going to a Club with their friends, I usually advice them to finish what they are drinking or take it with them when they are going to use the toilet because somebody might `lace` the drink with illegal substance.

When the children were young, alcoholic drinks used to be on our shopping list but when they reached their teens; I stopped buying them weekly because I want to teach my children by example.

Chapter Twenty-Three

Teenagers and Modern Technology

Teenagers of today are born into technological age with modern gadgets in their surroundings. I emphasize to my children not to let modern gadgets control them as they could easily lead to 'addictive behaviour'. There is a tendency for some parents to purchase television sets for their teenagers to watch in their bedrooms. This could become detrimental to the children's educational achievement.

Computer games, game boy and mobile have advantages and disadvantages. My last-born uses mobile phone to communicate with us at home if she is delayed on her way after school. Parents can use mobile phones to re-locate the whereabouts of the child too. However, care should be taken with their use and teenagers should be monitored and constantly reminded about the implications of long-term use of it. Currently, there is inconclusive evidence that long-term use of mobile phone generates radiation and its effect could damage the hearing of young people and teenagers; it is very expensive leisure in terms of mobile phone bills too!

The computer and television in the children bedrooms are disruptive and dangerous. By leaving children to stay on computer that could lead them to be a prey to a child molester or paedophiles; and they could be watching pornographic materials late in the hours, which could jeopardize their concentration in the classroom the following morning, especially during the week.

Computer games can become a habit forming for young children especially a young boy; hence, if a boy has a computer in his room, he can become addicted on the game and spend most of his time playing it without bothering to do his homework or read his books. To avoid that habit forming, my wife and I disagree with the idea of buying television or computer for the children to be used in their bedrooms. Bedrooms are created for people to sleep in and not to be used to distract ones sleeping patterns.

Therefore, our thirteen-year-old girl has not got a television or computer in her bedroom. She is only allowed a stereo. She is advised to spend less time on the computer in the dinning area. She became aware that I would question her activities on the computer if she stayed on it for too long because most of the time I am in the dinning table writing or reading newspapers. The family computer was in the living room so it could be easily monitored; now that she has left secondary school she can now be responsible enough to have a TV in her room.

She is allowed to own a mobile phone in order to communicate with my wife and I in case of emergencies. She is advised constantly to spend more time with her schoolwork than talking endlessly on the phone with her friends (which she does). When the bill arrives and it is higher than the previous one, she will be called to explain the reason. She is also reminded of the physical effect of spending too much time on the mobile and Internet because of the 'media' publicity about the radiation from especially mobile phones and 'addictive nature' of modern technology too.

I informed her that it is always dangerous to use the mobile phone in the rain and in stormy weathers when there is lighting and drew her attention to the latest research in the Lancet, British Medical Journal, about the dangers (2006)

Chapter Twenty-Four

"Clubbing" by Teenagers

My thirteen- year old girl informed me about a 'junior jam' with a number one, hip-hop and R'n'B singer from the United States of America, Lil Bow Wow. Choice FM organized the concert and it took place in Hammersmith Palais in 2005 between midday and 6pm one Saturday. She expressed her desire to attend the concert with her friends. She needed to buy the ticket in advance so I had to let her know whether my wife and I would allow her to attend the concert or not. I told her that I was going to discuss with her mother first and will think about it. She said it costs £10 per child. Two days later, I gave her the money to buy the ticket after consultation with my wife.

The reason why we gave her permission to go was three-fold: Firstly, it was geared towards her age group. Secondly, she was attending the concert with her cousin and friends from her school and thirdly, the concert were to end 6pm. Moreover, I did not want her to feel left out from this general social event, which has been widely advertised on the radio, in teenage magazines and newspapers.

I advised her on the day she was going that she should not take a drink being offered to her by her friends. I asked her: "Do you know sometimes friends could add strange substances to drinks at Night Club?" She replied: "I don't know". You should go with a bottle of water or she could buy one after the concert. I normally advise my older children not to leave their drinks behind when they are in a club and they are visiting the toilet. It is a place some people "lace" drinks for teenage girls and women to be intoxicated.

Her eldest sister went to pick her up on the way home. I asked her about her experience from the concert. She informed me that whilst walking towards the tube station, they saw a boy pulling a knife from his shoes. They had to take a shelter in a nearby W.H. Smith shop. I used the situation to remind her that due to that type of anti-social behaviour by some teenagers on the streets, that is why we feel reluctant to allow her to attend such concerts at certain time of the day. From that experience, she did not ask permission to go to such Concerts again.

My wife and I made sure that she had a structured life (being the last born in the family, there was the tendency to ignore her social life). Apart from attending school from Monday to Friday, she has extra classes to supplement her schoolwork especially in English language, Maths and Science every Saturday. On Sundays, we made sure that we attended church service together.

I asked her: "How do you find this routine?" She replied: "Alright". I said to her that life could be boring without structured daily activity for both the adult and teenager; therefore, she needs more disciplined and structured routine that would form the basis of her life style for the future. She said to me later that nowadays she looks forward to weekends.

Chapter Twenty-Five

Drug Education (Opiate) For Children and Teenagers

When my last child was ten years old in her last year of Primary Education, her teacher (a Deputy Headteacher) invited parents to come to her school to talk to the pupils about the work they do. My daughter came to tell me, as she knew I liked to take part in such activities. I volunteered to talk to the Primary pupils about illegal substances because she knows I work in the Specialist Addictive Behaviours Field with Masters Degree from St.George`s Hospital Medical School, which is part of University of London.

The occasion gave me the platform to give first hand information to the children aged between 9 and 11years old about the effects of drug use at this early stage of their lives. There were questions and answers and a quiz game at the end of the session. All the children and the teacher appreciated my input in bringing to the attention of pupils how illegal drug misuse such as heroin could have detrimental effect on their health.

I started with an explanation of how the opiates (heroin) a Class A drug, works on the brain. Endorphins are part of the body's pain killing and `feeling good` systems. Some believe that as opiates are much more powerful than endorphins, our natural pain killing agent, when one takes opiates (heroin), the body gives up the production of endorphins altogether; and when the person stops taking opiates, the endorphins production takes up to six months to return to normal levels.

Before endorphins production reverts to normality, the pain threshold becomes very low that one feels aches and pains easily when that person stops taking opiates. To avoid the pain, one needs to continue taking the opiates unless one undergoes detoxification programme at Drug Dependency Treatment Unit or rehabilitation clinic to recover from the addiction.

Heroin and opiate was first synthesized at the end of the 19th Century from Morphine, a substance extracted from the poppy plants (Opium). Heroin is known in the drug-using culture as: brown sugar, dope, brown sugar, gear, H, Jack, goop, scag, junk, horse, smack. It can be smoked or injected to produce a `rush`. First-time use of heroin can cause vomiting, nausea, severe headache and addiction.

Users sometimes experience a feeling of well-being, contentment and detachment from worries. Long-term effects of injecting heroin include collapsed veins and loss of appetite. Decade of abuse of heroin can destroy the veins of an arm. One can mistake capillary for a vein; and the drug can burn through them and lead to

Necrosis or dead flesh over the arms, which could lead to amputation.

It is expensive business to be addicted to opiates. Even if one is a multi-millionaire, one will eventually spend most of the money on these drugs.

Sooner or later one has to find the money to feed the habit in the form of committing crime like stealing and shoplifting. This behaviour pattern becomes a habit and the person is always involved with the police and eventually might spend greater part of his or her life in and out of the prison for illegal drug offences.

I wish to share the following poem with parents, Children and teenagers wherever they may be to illustrate how illegal substances like heroin could wreck their romantic, career, academic and sporting chances.

Riding White Horses

“Come ride the white horse. The horse dealer cried `you’ll have a great

trip`. He casually lied. The first ride’s free`. Those words done the trick .I rode off her back, but after felt sick. The next time I saw him, I asked after his horse. I wanted a ride and he said But of course. He charged me a £10,which seemed kind of mean. I rode to a heaven where I’d never been.

When the journey was over, the horse brought me back to a new hell on earth, where I needed more smack. I sought the horse dealer and begged him for more. My pride and £10 it cost me to score. The horse ran from heaven to hell with my soul. I`no longer the master, the horse had control.

The dealer looked different; horns, hoof and a tail, upon my return a guaranteed sale

Fixed up once to the heavens I rode. I tried chasing the dragons, but it cost me much gold. White horses cost plenty and my money had gone.

So I stole for my habit; but I knew it was wrong.

In prison, white horses are not allowed in .I shivered, grew sick and my body turned thin. That is the story of my horse riding days. Now I'm left with nothing; but memories don't haze. So if you ride the white horse, please ride it well. For the white horse of heroin will make your life hell"(By Daniel Marshall, unknown date).

My working experience in Addiction field has given me the first hand information about how substance misuse could ruin people's lives. People from all works of life could be inflicted with the problem of substance misuse today. Teenagers without skills, the youth who has started College or University course and successful businessmen and women and professional people could be involved in the illegal substance culture. As addiction is `chronic` relapsing condition, it becomes very difficult to come off from substances like alcohol, opiate, valium and crack- cocaine once you become addicted to them unless you undergo detoxification programme at Rehabilitation Unit. I share this information with my family and my children and draw their attention that there is widespread substance misuse in society today; and the outcome is detrimental to individual life.

Chapter Twenty-Six

State Primary/Secondary Schools and Educational Reforms

Placing a child into a good State Primary and Secondary schools in London is like a `lottery`. The parent needs to know what is happening in the education system. One has to do his or her homework well by reading the relevant Education sections of The Guardian, The Telegraph, The Independent, The Times and The Sunday Times regularly and attend the parent evenings of the child to listen and talk to the teachers and fellow parents.

For example, parents need to know that there are at least five categories of State Secondary Schools to choose their child's schools from if they have no money to send their child or children to a good Private or Independent Secondary School.

Faith Schools select their pupils on religious affiliation using Church attendance records, recommendations from Priests, Reverend Ministers, Immans, Primary Head teachers and parental interviews.

Grammar Schools select their pupils based on academic ability from across local authority areas. For example, if a child lives in any Borough, the child will sit for the School entrance test. Once he or she gets the required mark in the examination, the child could be admitted depending on the number of Children the School would accommodate during that year.

Academies set their own admission criteria in line with their own code of practice. They can select their percent of pupils on aptitude.

Specialists Schools can select their percent of pupils on aptitude in the Schools chosen specialization. For example, it could be in Science, ICT/Computing and Mathematics and Languages. Our last child, a girl, had admission into one of the Science Specialist Secondary Schools in Greater London.

Foundation/Voluntary-Aided Schools are free to set selection criteria as long as they comply with the Schools admission code of practice (The Guardian, 2005).

The system is complicated and complex that if a parent needs to send his or her child to a good State School, one has to do a lot of research. The distance between the child's home and the child's chosen School is vital, and if possible both the mother and father/partner should think very carefully about the location or area they wish to settle before becoming parents especially if they wish to send the child to Foundation/Voluntary-Aided Schools. It awards some places on the basis that a child has a sibling already in the School, has places based on ability and others on geographical distance. It has been noted that wealthy parents spend thousands of pounds to move into the catchment areas of the most successful Schools rather than pay for good Private School Fees, (The Guardian, 2005)

The amalgamation of GCE and CSE had implications for most parents too. For example, most of us are not aware that there are three Tiers, namely Higher Plus, Higher and Foundation Tiers especially in Mathematics, Science and Languages when Year 9 Students are selecting their Final GCSE Subjects

The Higher Plus Tier in GCSE allows the pupil to aim at A* A or B grades. GCSE Higher Tiers allows pupils to aim at D, C or B grades; and Foundation Tiers comprise F, E or D grades. The ability for parents to differentiate the three Tiers is crucial in order to know whether ones child would be able to achieve the `magic` band of A* to C grades at GCSE to undertake A Levels at the Sixth Form or College Of Further Education.

If the parent does not understand the Tiers and the child is placed in the Foundation Tier in Year 10,then the child may come out with qualifications which may jeopardise their further educational courses or career.

The child has to do remedial course or courses to compensate for that handicap to be able to be successful in the job market if he or she chooses to opt out for that route.

There is, however, G.N.V.Q, General National Vocational Qualifications in the Intermediate and

Advanced Levels Courses to upgrade the subjects if the child wants to pursue higher qualification or professions.

Because of the complexity of the education system and the reforms that is why parents have to get involve in their children education, talk with them, attend parental evenings, visit the Schools and volunteer in the Parents teacher Association. By so doing, parents will hear from the teachers about new developments and can ask the teachers the relevant questions about the child's achievement and progress, or ask other parents or share with them about their information they have on education system.

Above all, parents can always approach the head teachers with any problem regarding their child's education. During the recent Parent Evening at the Secondary School of my last child, I asked the Head of Science Department of the

School about the new General and Additional Science Syllabus. The question was

Based on whether the multiple-type questions for the General Science will start from Year 10 in 2006.By attending the Parent Evenings, the Head of the Science Department was able to give the right answers and further information about the changes in the GCSE Science syllabus in England.

Chapter Twenty-Seven

Career Guidance and Choice of University or College

Luckily, I have been through the tertiary Education system in Britain as a mature student. I have attended three former Polytechnics (now Universities), another College of Higher Education (now University) and St George's Hospital Medical School, part of University of London.

My children were encouraged to do well in all the subjects especially, English, Mathematics and Science subjects because they are essential for future studies. From Primary School till the Secondary school, my wife and I supplemented their work with extra tuition by enrolling them with Saturday Schools and personal tuition to assist them in their basic school subjects. I bought myself Mathematics books and I studied the traditional topics to be able to explain to the children in case they needed some support with their homework. I gave them advice about the choice of subjects and careers. They took my advice seriously because I used to invite them to my graduation ceremonies and so realised that my information is valid.

I studied the job market and tried to steer the children towards areas they could eventually obtain a reasonable job in future. During their school days, we got involved in finding work placement for them. When our son was in year 12 at Secondary School, his School found him work placement at an establishment unconnected with his future career plans. We trusted the School judgment to make informed decision on our behalf. We came to conclusion that we would get involve in the choice of our boy's work placement. The reason was that we wanted him to gain an experience in the field similar to his future career. I approached my dentist and informed him that my son wanted to work in science related industry and needed work experience. He agreed to let him work at his Practice during the Sixth Form Work Placement Period.

By knowing the strengths and weaknesses of the teenager, parents could be able to guide the teenager in the choice of his or her GCSE subjects, work placement, 'A' Level subjects and University Course. I took it upon myself to study most of the Education Sections of all the quality Newspapers in England.

Since 1992, I have been analysing the Times League Table of the Universities in the United Kingdom and I have come to conclusion that even though some Universities are famous and respected in the academic world; some courses taught in the departments of some former Polytechnics are equally popular and respected by many employers.

Writing in the Times Good University Guide (2004), Halpin points out that the position of some Newer Universities are lower in the League Table because such Institutions have far lower research assessment rating and spends small amount of money on student facilities. Nevertheless, their graduate employment record is better than some well-established, popular and respected Universities.

I advised my son to choose a Life Sciences degree Course at a former Polytechnic, now a University in London. He asked me the reason why he should do the course. I told him that undertaking degree in Life Sciences would open more avenues to science-related career opportunities in future. When he completed the Course, he was able to secure a job in the same field. The Department he pursued his degree once placed higher than some of the well-established Universities; and it ranked amongst the top 20 Universities in that discipline (2004).

Our eldest daughter attended a former Polytechnic to do a Combined degree in Law; and one of her tutors at the Law Department had written a book on Land Law which is popular and widely read by Law students at every College or University in the UK. When undertaking her Post-Graduate Diploma in Legal Practice (LPC) course at another former Polytechnic, she met other Students doing the same Course who had attended Russell Universities. Most of the Post Graduate

Diploma in Legal Practice course is carried out in the former Polytechnics.

Even though well-established institutions have the advantage over the modern universities, individual departments at various Universities also have potential. London South Bank University placed seventh in the highest graduate starting salaries, according to the Sunday Times, University Guide (2006).

Warwick, Bath and York were established in the sixties, but they are among the top ten best-researched Universities in the UK. In short, every University that appears in the League Table of the quality Newspapers in the UK has its strengths and weaknesses. It is up to the parents to study the trend of the Universities through the yearly League Tables in the Guardian, the Times and Sunday Times and the Independent.

Writing in the Rise, Saturday Guardian, 21st January 2006,David Williams quoted Mick Hill, Chief Director of Graduate Prospects saying "…great majority of students go into jobs that are nothing to do with blue-chip companies and points out that it does not matter what University you go to". Hill, however, points out that " …the evidence seems to show that if one wants to get a job with one of the major Graduate recruiters, the one that dominate the press, it does matter what University one went to".

Parents should therefore discuss with the teenager whether he or she wants to go to College or University because at the end of the day, the responsibility rests on the teenager. They should weigh the cost of the studies against the prospect of paying the debts at the end of the three years and beyond. There is no point for a teenager to do a course and drop out.

Recent survey of future employers indicates that skills in electrical work, plumbing, social and health care, hairdressing would be in great demand in future. Therefore, children should consider such skills when they are thinking of their career plans in future. Parents should know the strengths and weaknesses of their teenager. If a teenager is academically bright, then of course, he or she should be encouraged to go to University to do a career-orientated degree. If he or she is not, then the parent should channel the teenager to learn a trade in any of the shortage skill areas like Information and Communication Technology, Carpentry, Bricklaying, Hospitality, Painting and decorating, Hairdressing, Plumbing and Electrical courses at a Local College. Opportunities are available at the moment for teenagers to acquire these skills, which could enable them to secure a job without relying on the Welfare State for their financial needs.

Chapter Twenty-Eight

Conclusion

I have taken readers on a journey of parenting children and teenagers based on my personal experience in Britain. It has been a hard work and a struggle with my wife. There were trials and tribulations during this process. I agree with Ironside (2006), the Agony Aunt, that" any fool can get a degree, but not everyone can be a good mother (father), simply because it's one of the most demanding and important jobs in the world".

Financing the University and Professional Education of the three children especially in their twenties was full of distress but it was worth it. On a happy note, the eldest child, a girl, has qualified as a Solicitor, the second child, the only son, is a graduate in the Life Sciences and has gained a professional qualification in his chosen field; and now works with a multi-national company; our third child, a girl, has graduated recently with a Law Degree from a Russell University; and the last child, a girl is in year ten at Secondary School (2005).

Unlike my teenage years in Africa, we did not receive a helping hand from our grandparents in bringing up our four children in the United Kingdom. There were conflicts as in all marriages. It soon dawned on my wife and I that compromises in the marriage and parenting are crucial qualities. During the course of parenting, there are issues, which need to be sorted out between the woman and the man if they are to succeed in their objectives.

For example, when the children were young, they used to like the idea of sleeping over in their friends' houses. I did not believe in this idea so I used to refuse the children spending the night in their friends' houses. This led to some conflicts but it was resolved by discussion and compromises with my wife. Eventually, it was agreed that once a child's family is familiar to both of us, perhaps, then our child could be allowed to sleep over. My wife and I made it known to our children that their friends could rather visit or sleep over in our home if they wish.

On discipline, we adopted a firm, fair and consistent method. We realized that whenever one of us is reprimanding one of the children, none of us should interfere with each other. For example, if my wife is reprimanding one of the children for being disobedient, I made sure that I allowed her to do so. If I did not agree with her in the first place, I usually drew her attention to this after she had disciplined the child, and when the child or children are not around.

If a child asks for anything, my wife and I would discuss and then come to compromise decision before giving in to the child. Whatever decision is taken, I supported this, as did my wife.

Childcare and parenting are very expensive and costly business. Quoting a recent survey, Bennett (2006) point out that the cost of raising a child is rising faster than property prices, and is now almost as expensive as buying a house outright. The survey points out that raising one child from birth to the age of 21(graduate level) costs £180,137 if the child is State educated. We soon realized that double income couples are consistently better off than couples with few skills or qualifications. The latter parents are materially disadvantaged in a consumer society like Britain. Therefore, parents need to get a skill or skills to be able to secure a reasonable job in society in order to be able to provide the basic needs, childcare and University education for the child or children. We therefore, had to train and re-train in various skills in order to achieve different skills to be able to get secured jobs.

In order to educate, train and re-train, parents need to sacrifice and forgo certain material possessions. I soon realized that instead of buying expensive clothes and shoes as I used to do when I was single, I began to buy clothes from budget shops or did not buy unnecessary clothes unless there was a need to do so. Moreover, I realized that I had to avoid the `rat-race` and the phenomena of `keeping up with the Jones` too. Instead, I focused on my children's educational needs. I would rather use my money to buy a book or books for the children than to spend it on myself. I advised the children to aim high so that they could achieve more laurels in their chosen professions or fields than I was able to.

In retrospect, every disciplinary measure taken against the children were made in consultation with my wife to avoid conflict and prevent any room of manipulation from the child or children.

With reference to London School boy stabbing (2006) and shooting (2006) by fellow teenagers, one legacy parents should reinforce in their teenagers is that they should be law-abiding citizens. To do that, parents should stress to their teenagers the need to focus on their studies and avoid joining gangs who cause trouble outside and inside School playing grounds. Parents should set good example for their children to emulate by spending more time with them. Mothers in general and fathers in particular need to work hard to steer their teenagers away from the knife and gun culture and other anti-social behaviour at an early stage of a child's life.

My four children have now grown into well-rounded individuals. At the time of going to the publishers (2010), my eldest daughter is 32 years of age, the second born, the boy, is 29 years, the third born is 25 years and they are working in their respective chosen professions. The last born who is in her teens passed her GCE Advanced levels few days before her eighteenth birthday. She is now an undergraduate science student at the University of Hertfordshire.

Bibliography

Books quoted in the text

Coser, Lewis (1956)
The Functions of Social Conflict
(Routledge & Kegan Paul)

Dearlove, John & Saunders, Peter (1986)
Introduction to British Politics
(Polity Press)

The Holy Bible (1976)
Proverbs Chapter 13 verse 24
Authorised King James Version
Bible House Charlotte
North Carolina,USA

O'Leary, John & Kingston Bernard (2005)
The Times Good University Guide
Times Books 12th edition

Hoper Collins-London
Sealy, Hope (1989)
Prayer for the day, BBC Books, London

Strathern, Paul (1999)
The Essential Confucius
Virgin Books Ltd, London

Warner, Judith (2005)
Project madness (motherhood in the age of Anxiety)
Ebury

Articles Quoted in the Text

1. Beckett, Francis (2005)
   Baby boomers head for flower
   Power struggle, The Guardian

2. Blunett, John (2005)
   Minority Report
   Media Guardian

3. Bennett,Rosemary
   `Cost of raising a child hits £180,000 Times 10th
   November 2006

4. Cassidy, Sara (2006)
   Troubled marriages hold back pupils
   Education correspondent, The Independent

5. Campbell, Sara & Roberts, Celia (2006)
   Selective hearing
   People Management
   Personnel Publications Ltd, London

6. Dobson, Roger & Swinford, Steven
Delmar-Morgan, Alex (2006)
British children among Europe's most deprived
The Sunday Times

7. Halpin, Tony (2005)
The Good University Guide

8. Ironside, Virginia (2006)
The Agony Aunt
Daily Mail

9. Lister, Sam (2006)
Lighting peril for Mobile phones in a storm
The Times

10 Martin, Paul (2005)
Being happy is child's play
The Sunday Times

11. Matthew, David (2004)
The Trouble with Black Men
The Sunday Times

12. Murray, Charles (2005)
The Advantages of Social apartheid
The Sunday Times

13. Taylor, Matthew (2006)
Minister plans to improve pupils' exam results
The Guardian Correspondent

14 Taylor, Matthew (2005)
Top State Schools Colonised by middle classes
The Guardian

15. Nugent, Helen (2006)
Boy stabbed outside School
The Times

16. X, Malcolm (1965)
Tomorrow belongs to those who prepare for it today.

17. Diversity news in brief
Work Experience (2006)
The Independent

18. Wedding rows (2006)
The Times

19. University Guide (2006)
The Sunday Times

20 The Return of the Family (1993)
The Sunday Times (Editorial)

21. What your child could be up to the facts (2005)
The BBC-Frank Raising Kids

22. Slack, James (2006)
One in five pupils have been lured into drugs.
Daily Mail

23. Henderson, Mark (2006)
Cannabis "Gateway " to addiction
The Times

24. And in case you have forgotten
The Ten Commandments
Daily Express (2004)

25. Evans, Amanda (2006)
"My guilt, by dad of gang murder Alex"
News of the World (June 18th, 2006)

26. Shooting of black 17 year old in Brixton, London (28/09/2006)

Glossary

1. Riding white horses –injecting China white or heroin
2. Horse-heroin
3. Hooked-addicted
4. Chasing the dragons-inhaling fumes of heated heroin on the foil
5. Score-inject
6. Smack-heroin

About the Author

Owusu Ansa Boafo was born in Ghana and trained as a psychiatric and general nurse at St David`s Hospital in Carmarthen, South West Wales and St James`s University Hospital in Leeds, Yorkshire respectively.

He later studied Higher National Diploma in Business Studies with Personnel Option at Huddersfield University,Post Diploma in Personnel Management at the Regional Management Centre, Kingston University, Surrey, and passed the professional examination of the Charted Institute of Personnel and Development (CIPD), Degree in Social Sciences and Masters Degree in Sociology at London South Bank University, Counselling at Roehampton University, London and Masters Degree in Addictive Behaviour at St George's Hospital Medical School, part of University of London.

He is currently working in the Addictive Behaviour field at Springfield University Hospital in South London. He has also worked as a Residential Social Worker, a Teacher and briefly as a Personnel Officer in Britain.

He lives in London with his wife and four children.

ND - #0254 - 080726 - C0 - 197/132/11 - PB - 9781844268948 - Gloss Lamination